Millennium Kopprasch Series
Duet Kopprasch
Vol. I

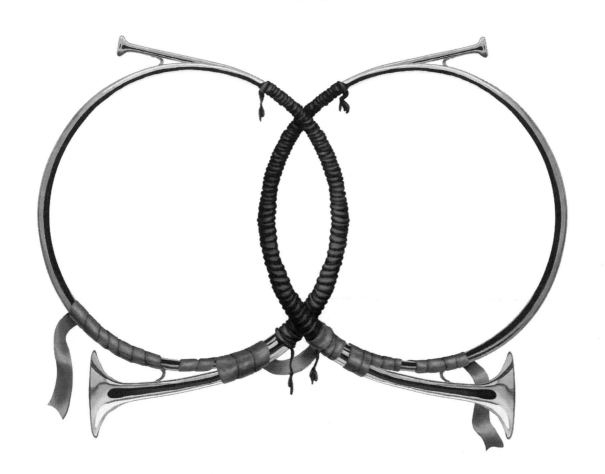

Jeffrey Agrell

Copyright © 2018 by Jeffrey Agrell

All rights reserved. No part of this book, including interior design, cover design, logos, and icons may be reproduced or transmitted in any form, by any means (electronic, photocopying, recording, or otherwise) without the prior consent of the publisher except for brief quotations in a book review. "Wildwind Editions" and the Wildwind Editions logo are trademarks of Wildwind Editions.

Published by Wildwind Editions
Cover art by Karin Wittig
Layout and formatting by Awadhesh Yadav

First Printing: 2018

ISBN-13: 978-1722175719
ISBN-10: 1722175719

Books by Jeffrey Agrell

Preparatory Kopprasch

Harmony Kopprasch

Rhythm Kopprasch

Horn Technique

The Creative Hornist

Improvisation Games for Classical Musicians (2008)

Improvisation Games for Classical Musicians, Vol. II (2016)

Improvised Chamber Music for Classical Musicians

Improv Games for One Player

Improv Duets for Classical Musicians

Vocal Improvisation Games
(with co-author Patrice Madura)

Creative Pedagogy for Piano Teachers
(with co-author Aura Strohschein)

The Millennium Kopprasch Series

I know what you're thinking: What? Messing with Kopprasch? Why? Is that even legal? Or, alternatively, you might be thinking: It's about time someone did an update!

Good questions! What we familiarly and simply call "Kopprasch" refers to the etude collection of 60 studies for low horn Op. 6 by German composer Georg Kopprasch (ca. 1800 - c. 1850). Kopprasch was a professional hornist whose career included playing in the Royal Berlin Theater Orchestra (after 1822) and the court orchestra of the Prince of Dessau (after 1832). His sixty etudes (commonly published in two volumes) were some of the earliest etudes published for the newly invented valve horn, and are still arguably the most popular etudes for horn (as well as being regularly poached by other brasses) today.

The etudes are often quite "mechanical" in nature (with a couple of exceptions), and are essentially various elaborations of the most basic musical material: scales and arpeggios. All well and good, and still useful today, but there is one inescapable problem: a few things have changed in both the real and the musical world since the early 19th century. It goes without saying (so we will say it): the musician of the new millennium can expect to face technical and musical challenges that far exceed the basics covered by Kopprasch.

What we do in The Millennium Kopprasch Series is to take the familiar and stretch it, that is, we take Kopprasch's etudes and dramatically add challenges to them in various ways so that the millennium musician acquires the depth and breadth they need to survive and thrive almost two hundred years after those first original etudes were written. Look around: how many things do you see are the same as they were in 1830? Transportation. Food. Science. Communication. Clothing. Musical styles. Medicine. Sports. Anything electric. And on and on. It requires no great effort to see the tremendous differences. Hence this series, which simply asks: *shouldn't musical studies reflect the demands of the current era?*

The Millennium Kopprasch Series will (theoretically) eventually comprise about ten two-volume sets of Kopprasch (heretofore our shorthand term for the etude collection), in two volumes for each version to mirror the originals. *Rhythm Kopprasch* was the first of these re-imagined etudes, then *Harmony Kopprasch*, *Prepartory Kopprasch*, and *Duet Kopprasch* here. Subsequent volumes will appear every few months for the next several years. Stay tuned, and be the first on your block to collect the entire series!

PS: send us your email address if you would like to be informed when the next set is published: jeffrey.agrell@gmail.com

Duet Kopprasch

The standard paradigm of a classical musician's practice is very much akin to the lot of a monk in a monastery – you spend most of your time in a tiny room, repeating certain rituals that will supposedly produce beneficial personal results. The fact is that almost all technique can be profitably practiced with a partner. At the very least it makes the time pass much more quickly, and you will quickly discover that practicing technique *a due* is much more fun and more productive. Instead of the usual enforced isolation and privation, technique is now social, motivating, and challenging.

Sage Stephen Nachmanovitch says this:

> *One advantage of collaboration is that it's much easier to learn from someone else than from yourself. And inertia, which is often a major block in solitary work, hardly exists at all here; you release each other's energy. Learning becomes many-sided, a refreshing and vitalizing force.*

In a word: fun!

I know, I know, music (study) is serious! No having fun! But just this once, I give you permission to enjoy yourself while working on that beneficial but bitter medicine known as Kopprasch. The challenges of the duet version are no less (sometimes more and sometimes different) than the original, but since you are in this together, the Sisyphean task of pushing the heavy boulder of technique study up the endless "hill" is transformed into more of an exhilarating downhill toboggan ride.

A word about the duets: in almost all cases in this volume, the original line has been shared in various ways between the two voices, principally for musical reasons. For some reason, Kopprasch, like so many composers of etudes of that era, decided that horn etudes should look like violin etudes – an endless rata tat tat continuous blizzard of notes without regard for that basic feature of carbon-based life forms: having to breathe occasionally. OK, sometimes music looks like that, but mostly it doesn't. We decided to make it look more like most music, to feature more counterpoint, more interwoven lines that are both more fun to play and interesting to listen to. We also add some rhythmic fun in the accompaniment in various places for lagniappe.

In any case, have fun playing some K in this new duet setting. Really – it's ok to have fun with these. We won't tell. The folks out in the hall outside your practice room won't know either – they simply won't recognize the old barn burners in this new setting. Feel free to add percussion...

Millennium Kopprasch Series
Duet Kopprasch
Vol. I

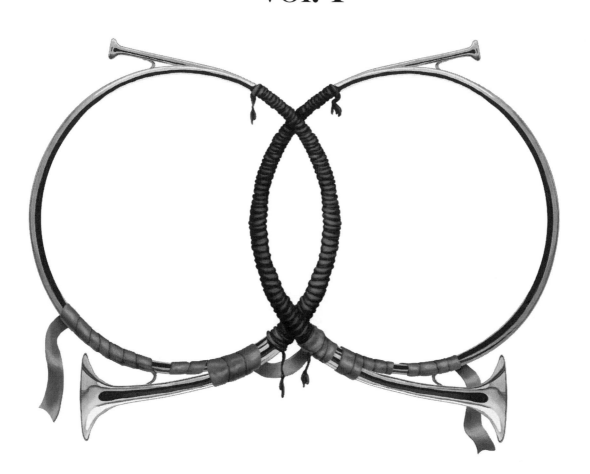

Jeffrey Agrell

Duet Kopprasch Etudes

1

3

4

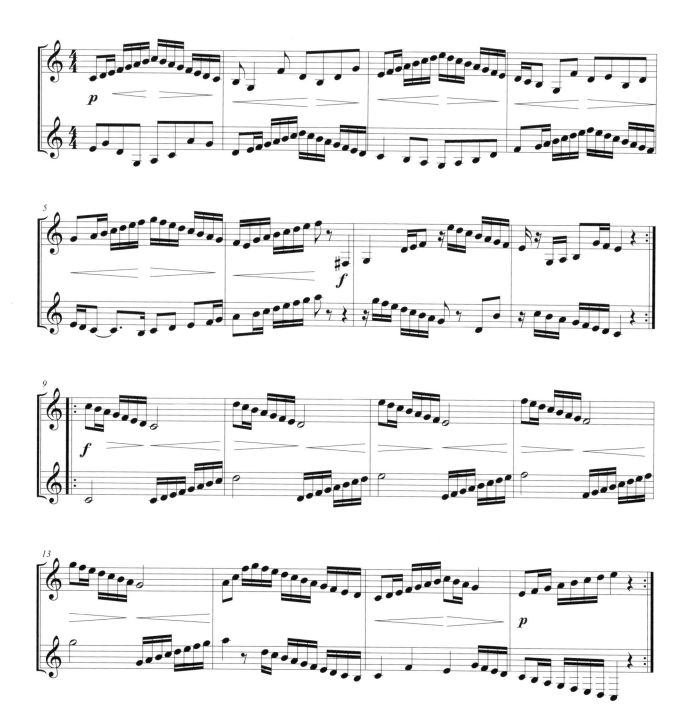

5

6

7

8

9

10

[No. 11 - omitted]

12

13

15

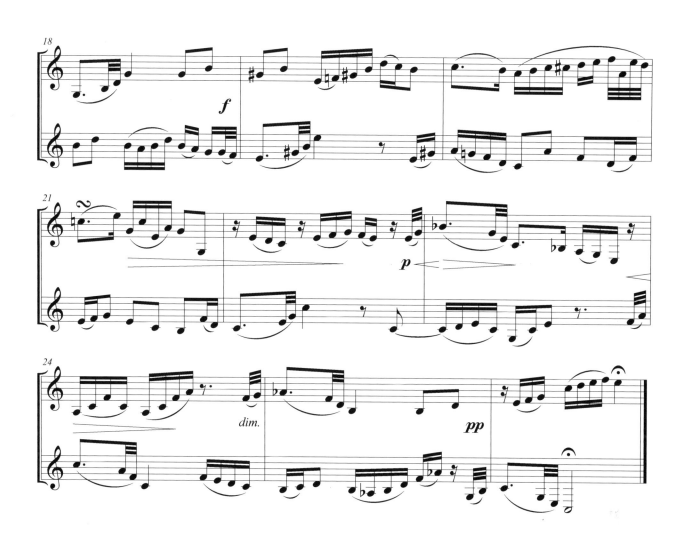

16

17

18

19

21

22

23

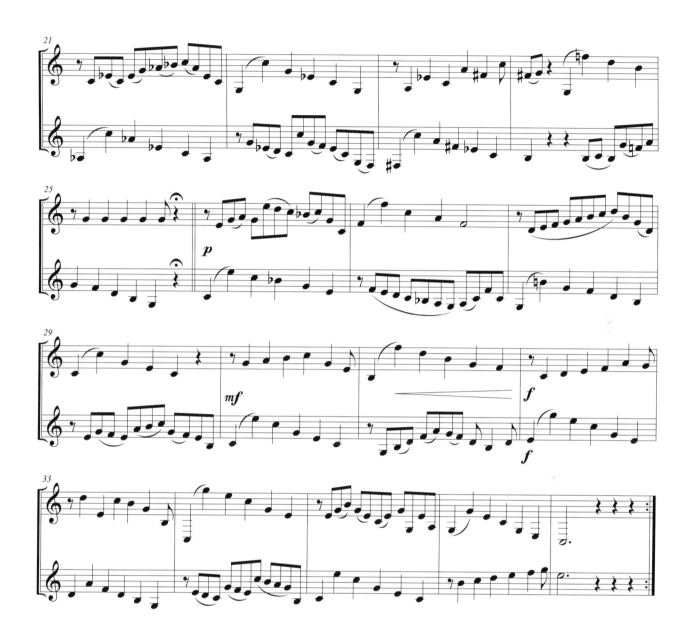

24

25

26

27

28

29

30

31

32

34

About the Author

Jeffrey Agrell has earned his living playing and teaching horn since college. After a first career as a symphony orchestra musician, he has been horn professor at the University of Iowa since 2000.

He has performed and taught the full gamut of horn literature, including the repertoire for symphony orchestra, opera, musicals, ballet, operetta, and chamber music, while stretching personal artistic boundaries beyond the orchestra as a educator, composer, writer, clinician, recording artist, and solo performer. He is a former two-term member of the Advisory Council of the International Horn Society, has been a member of the faculty of the Asian Youth Orchestra in Hong Kong, and has taught at the prestigious Kendall Betts Horn Camp since 2005.

Besides performing, he has won awards as both a writer and composer, with well over one hundred published articles, dozens of published and recorded compositions, and many books to his credit, most recently, the Millennium Kopprasch Series *(Duet Kopprasch, Preparatory Kopprasch, Rhythm Kopprasch, Harmony Kopprasch)*, Horn Technique (447 p., 2017) and *The Creative Hornist* (228 p., 2017). He is an expert on classical improvisation, and has authored landmark books in this area, including *Improvisation Games for Classical Musicians*, Vol. I (2008) and Vol. II (2016).

Outside of horn and writing, he is a used-to-be amateur jazz guitarist, and currently an enthusiastic, if not particularly skilled conga drum player.

To contact Jeffrey Agrell with questions, comments, crazy ideas, get into interesting discussions about any of this, or engage him for concerts, workshops, keynote addresses, lectures, masterclasses, and all that, write to him at jeffrey.agrell@gmail.com

Made in the USA
Middletown, DE
26 August 2022